HAIL TO THE CHIEF!

Make Me Laugh!

HAIL TO THE CHIEF!

jokes about the presidents

by Diane & Clint Burns/pictures by Joan Hanson

Lerner Publications Company • Minneapolis

To Victor Paulos and Ralph Greinke, who teach history (and more) with humor and love— D.L.B.

To Chris Tribbett— C.P.B.

Library of Congress Cataloging-in-Publication Data

Burns, Diane L.
  Hail to the chief!

  (Make me laugh!)
  Summary: A collection of jokes about the Presidents
and aspects of our political system.
    1. Presidents—United States—Juvenile humor.
2. Wit and humor, Juvenile. [1. Presidents—Wit and
humor. 2. Politics, Practical—Wit and humor.
3. Jokes] I. Burns, Clint. II. Hanson, Joan, ill.
III. Title. IV. Series.
PN6231.P693B87   1988   818'.5402   88-13133
ISBN 0-8225-0971-7 (lib. bdg.)

Manufactured in the United States of America

1 2 3 4 5 6 7 8 9 10 98 97 96 95 94 93 92 91 90 89

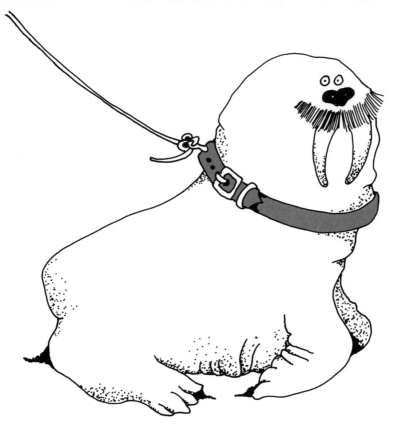

Q: Why does the president keep a pet walrus?
A: It's the great seal of the United States.

Q: Which president daydreamed?
A: George Wishing-ton.

Q: How does the president find his seat in a darkened theater?
A: Mon-row at a time.

Q: What fruit grows in the White House orchard?
A: Adams' apples.

Q: Which president liked to cook?
A: Thomas Chef-ferson.

Q: What kind of lawn grows on Capitol Hill?
A: Con-grass.

Q: Which president played in the dirt?
A: James Muddy-son.

Q: Which president did the most laundry?
A: Washing-ton.

Q: Who were the two smallest presidents?
A: John Atoms and John Quincy Atoms.

Q: Where do baby alphabet letters become larger?

A: On "Capitol" Hill.

Q: What music do senators listen to?
A: Anything played on congressional records.

Q: Who referees congressional football games?
A: A punt-agon official.

Q: How do members of congress play tennis?
A: With an inaugural ball.

Q: What do senators do at the Olympics?
A: They set congressional records.

Q: What do you call the braces on senators' teeth?

A: Congressional "metals."

Q: Which first lady was a perfect hostess?
A: Millard's wife Abigail, because she always knew when to Fill-more goblets.

Q: What dance is the president's favorite?
A: The James K. Polk-a.

Q: Who irons the president's shirt?
A: His "press" secretary.

Q: Which president made his own clothes?
A: Zachary Tailor.

Q: Whose favorite holiday was Halloween?
A: James Boo-chanan.

Q: Why does the president collect four-leaf clovers?

A: To help his next e-luck-tion.

Q: Who was the "sharpest" president?

A: Franklin Pierce.

Q: Which president read a lot of fiction?

A: James Book-chanan.

Q: Where does the president keep important papers?

A: In his Cabinet.

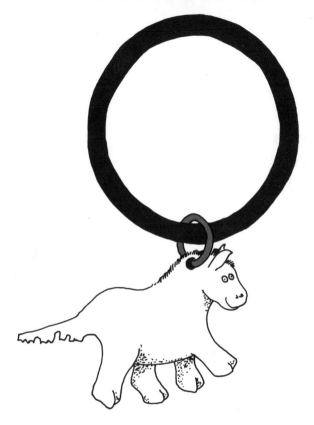

Q: How do Democrats lock their houses?
A: With a don-key.

Q: Which president drew lots of pictures?
A: Ulysses S. Crayont.

Q: Which president owned a supermarket?
A: Grocer Cleveland.

Q: What did presidents eat for breakfast during the Civil War?
A: Sausage Link-ons.

Q: What celebrations do Republicans and Democrats enjoy most?
A: Their political parties.

Q: What kind of trousers do Republicans wear?
A: Ele-pants.

Q: What do presidents eat during elections?
A: Candied-dates.

Q: Which president's car was the fanciest?
A: Lincoln's Continental.

Q: Where do presidents shop for used automobiles?
A: In a James A. Car-field.

Q: Which president discovered a fogger for beekeepers?
A: Rutherford's Bee-Haze.

Q: What did the political candidate get when he slept in a tent?

A: His presidential camp-pain.

Q: What did the hippies say who were hired to work on the White House roof?

A: "Man, is this a Calvin Cool-ledge!"

Q: What presidential vacuum cleaner is displayed in the Smithsonian Institution?

A: Herbert's Hoover.

Q: Where do members of Congress go at midnight?

A: To a secret service.

Q: Which president would you find inside a lawyer's file cabinet?

A: Woodrow Will-son.

Q: What did Shakespeare write about a sad president?

A: "Harding is such sweet sorrow..."

Q: How do presidents make old-fashioned candy in the White House?

A: They have a Taft-y pull.

√ **Q:** How did the blind man know he was in the White House flowergarden?

A: By the Theodore Rose-he-felt.

Q: What do you call a political rally for crows?
A: A caw-cus.

Q: Which president was always right?
A: Harry S. True-man.

Q: Why does the president's plane always land safely?
A: Because of Dwight's Eyes-in-tower.

Q: How does a candidate catch trout?
A: With a fishing poll.

Q: What spice do presidents use?
A: Ronald's O-Reagan-o.

Q: Why did the fisherman go to the trout stream on election day?

A: To "cast" his ballot.

Q: Which president's family was never poor?
A: Gerald's, because they only bought what they could af-Ford.

Q: Which president changed hairstyles?
A: Jimmy Parter.

Q: What weapon will presidents use in outer space?
A: A Ray-gun.

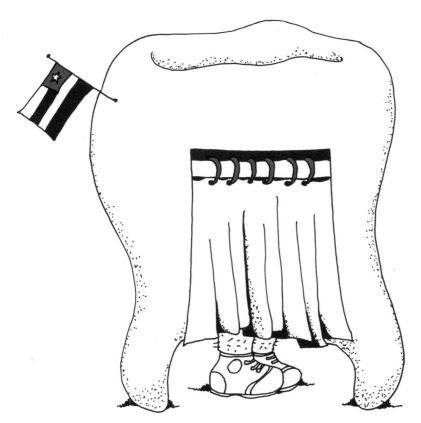

Q: Where does a dentist go during an election?
A: To a voting tooth.

Presidents of the United States

1. George Washington 1789-1797
2. John Adams 1797-1801
3. Thomas Jefferson 1801-1809
4. James Madison 1809-1817
5. James Monroe 1817-1825
6. John Quincy Adams 1825-1829
7. Andrew Jackson 1829-1837
8. Martin Van Buren 1837-1841
9. William Henry Harrison 1841
10. John Tyler 1841-1845
11. James K. Polk 1845-1849
12. Zachary Taylor 1849-1850
13. Millard Fillmore 1850-1853
14. Franklin Pierce 1853-1857
15. James Buchanan 1857-1861
16. Abraham Lincoln 1861-1865
17. Andrew Johnson 1865-1869
18. Ulysses S. Grant 1869-1877
19. Rutherford B. Hayes 1877-1881
20. James A. Garfield 1881

21. Chester Alan Arthur 1881-1885
22. Grover Cleveland 1885-1889
23. Benjamin Harrison 1889-1893
24. Grover Cleveland 1893-1897
25. William McKinley 1897-1901
26. Theodore Roosevelt 1901-1909
27. William Howard Taft 1909-1913
28. Woodrow Wilson 1913-1921
29. Warren G. Harding 1921-1923
30. Calvin Coolidge 1923-1929
31. Herbert Hoover 1929-1933
32. Franklin D. Roosevelt 1933-1945
33. Harry Truman 1945-1953
34. Dwight Eisenhower 1953-1961
35. John F. Kennedy 1961-1963
36. Lyndon B. Johnson 1963-1969
37. Richard Nixon 1969-1974
38. Gerald Ford 1974-1977
39. Jimmy Carter 1977-1981
40. Ronald Reagan 1981-1989

ABOUT THE AUTHORS

DIANE L. BURNS, her son, CLINT, and their family spend their summers "on top of the world" as firetower lookouts in Idaho's River-of-No-Return Wilderness. During the rest of the year, they manage a maple sugar farm outside Minneapolis, Minnesota. A former sixth grade teacher, Diane spends her free time writing stories for children and sharing food and laughter with friends. Clint, a junior-high student, enjoys fly fishing, bicycling, and basketball.

ABOUT THE ARTIST

JOAN HANSON lives with her husband and two sons in Afton, Minnesota. Her distinctive, deliberately whimsical pen-and-ink drawings have illustrated more than 30 children's books. Hanson is also an accomplished weaver. A graduate of Carleton College, Hanson enjoys tennis, skiing, sailing, reading, traveling, and walking in the woods surrounding her home.

Make Me Laugh!

CAN YOU MATCH THIS!
CAT'S OUT OF THE BAG!
CLOWNING AROUND!
DUMB CLUCKS!
ELEPHANTS NEVER FORGET!
FACE THE MUSIC!
FOSSIL FOLLIES!

GO HOG WILD!
GOING BUGGY!
GRIN AND BEAR IT!
HAIL TO THE CHIEF!
IN THE DOGHOUSE!
KISS A FROG!
LET'S CELEBRATE!
OUT TO LUNCH!
OUT TO PASTURE!
SNAKES ALIVE!
SOMETHING'S FISHY!
SPACE OUT!
STICK OUT YOUR TONGUE!
WHAT A HAM!
WHAT'S YOUR NAME?
WHAT'S YOUR NAME, AGAIN?
101 ANIMAL JOKES
101 FAMILY JOKES
101 KNOCK-KNOCK JOKES
101 MONSTER JOKES
101 SCHOOL JOKES
101 SPORTS JOKES